chase
study.

chasing after the heart of God

jennie allen

THOMAS NELSON
Since 1798

NASHVILLE   DALLAS   MEXICO CITY   RIO DE JANEIRO

Published in Nashville, Tennessee, by Thomas Nelson. Thomas Nelson is a registered trademark of Thomas Nelson, Inc.

Unless otherwise noted, Scripture quotations are taken from THE ENGLISH STANDARD VERSION. © 2001 by Crossway Bibles, a division of Good News Publishers.

Scripture quotations marked NIV are from the HOLY BIBLE: NEW INTERNATIONAL VERSION®. © 1973, 1978, 1984 by International Bible Society. Used by permission of Zondervan Publishing House. All rights reserved.

Thomas Nelson, Inc., titles may be purchased in bulk for educational, business, fund-raising, or sales promotional use. For information, please e-mail SpecialMarkets@ThomasNelson.com.

Author image © Jessica Taylor. Used with permission.

978-1-4185-4935-0

Printed in the United States of America

14 15 16 17 RRD 12 11 10 9 8

She will chase after her lovers but not catch them; she will look for them but not find them.

hosea 2:7 NIV

contents

introduction

I was eighteen years old. I felt paralyzed in my relationship with God. I knew God was real, but my fancy prayers and daily devotionals were not cutting it. I was doing everything right, but it felt all wrong. Yet I thought I was giving God what He wanted.

I began to question—and this good little Bible-belt girl somehow missed the rules for wrestling with her God. As I surveyed my life, I realized doing all the right things had won me the admiration of everyone but God. And I felt empty and prideful. It was worse than rebellion: being good with no God. It was beginning to occur to me maybe God was after something else.

Maybe I was chasing the wrong things.

And then I stumbled across a phrase in 1 Samuel 13.

David was "a man after [God's] own heart" (v. 14).

The phrase intrigued me because I knew David committed murder and adultery—he was no missionary or priest. I saw this man as both completely sold out for God and completely broken. He was in love with God. He lived with an acute awareness of his need for Him.

The closer I have gotten to the life of this man, David, the more my ideas of what God wants from me have been shattered. David had one life and two eyes and one heart, just like me, but they were all laser-focused on the heart of his God . . . my God. David was in love with Him.

And, yes, David sinned and wrestled, just like me. But while he was not so concerned about appearing godly, he was terribly concerned about knowing God. He was a man who saw past his circumstances, past himself, past this life to the heart of God.

We gather together to discover the heart of God.

I am terrified we get it wrong a lot of the time. We rarely, in our busy lives, stop and see Him, *really* see Him. We are so busy doing things for Him and for everyone else we altogether miss Him. He wants *us*.

As we chase after His heart together for these few short weeks, we will explore the life of David, a man who knew the heart of God. We will look into their passionate conversations. And whether you are running from God or working your tail off to please Him, David's journey will challenge your view of God.

The story of David's life and his prayers fill God's Word. It's as if God was saying, *When you open My Word, look at this man, look at his prayers, look at his life, look at his mistakes, look at his faith, and you'll see Me, My heart.*

Let's chase.

Jennie

instructions and expectations

What do you hope to get out of this study?

Engage with Your Small Group

An important part of personal growth is community. We are going to deal with the way we view God and how our hearts can change to be more like His. This could be a painful process and it will certainly reveal sin in all of us. Make sure you have a group of women to walk through this process with you.

Commit to Being Consistent and Present

The nature of life makes it nearly impossible to follow through with a thorough examination of our hearts and Scripture—not to mention the devil's desire to interfere with it. Commit to being present at your group meetings, barring an emergency, and arrange your schedule so you do not miss any part in this journey. Have your lesson and projects finished when you come to the group meeting.

Ground Rules
for Group Discussion Time

:: *Be concise.* Share your answers to the questions while protecting others' time for sharing. Be thoughtful. Don't be afraid to share with the group, but try not to dominate the conversation.

:: *Keep group members' stories confidential.* Many things your group members share are things they are choosing to share with you, not with your husband or other friends. Protect each other by not allowing anything shared in the group to leave the group.

:: *Rely on Scripture for truth.* We are prone to use conventional, worldly wisdom as truth. While there is value in that, this is not the place. If you feel led to respond, please only respond with God's truth and Word, not "advice."

:: *No counseling.* Protect the group by not directing all attention on solving one person's problem. This is the place for confessing and discovery and applying truth together as a group. Your group leader will be able to direct you to more help outside the group time if you need it. Don't be afraid to ask for help.

Study Design

In the first meeting, your groups' study guides will be passed out and you will work through the Getting Started lesson together. After that, each lesson in the study guide is meant to be completed on your own during the week before coming to the group meeting.

These lessons may feel different from studies you have done in the past. They are very interactive. The beginning of each lesson will involve you, your Bible, and a pen, working through Scripture and listening to God's voice. Each lesson will conclude with four projects you can do to help you further process how to live God's Word. Don't feel as if each lesson has to be finished in one sitting; take a few blocks of time throughout the week if you need to.

The goal of this study is to dig deeply into Scripture and uncover how it applies to your life, *to deeply engage the mind and the heart.* Projects, stories, and Bible study all play a role in it. You may be drawing or journaling or interacting with the homeless. At each group meeting you will discuss your experience in working through that week's lesson.

Terrific Resources for Further Personal Study

http://www.biblegateway.com/
http://www.bestcommentaries.com/

Who Is David and Why Does He Matter?

A. Who was David in history?

1. David was the second king of Israel.

2. He is said to have lived around 1040–970 BC.

3. His reign lasted a total of forty years.

4. David made Jerusalem the capital of Israel after he defeated the Jebusites who inhabited it.

5. David's reign can be divided into two segments. For the first seven years he reigned over Judah because the nation of Israel had been divided into two parts: Israel in the north and Judah in the south. Eventually, the kingdom was reunited and David reigned over it for thirty-three years.

B. Who is David in Scripture?

1. David is a king in the Old Testament. His life is primarily documented in 1 and 2 Samuel, concluding in 1 Kings.

2. At first, David was a shepherd, the youngest son of Jesse. However, God withdrew His favor from the current king, King Saul, and chose David to be the new king. God accomplished this by sending His prophet, Samuel, to choose a new king from among Jesse's sons.

3. David became Saul's armor-bearer. He then made a name for himself by defending Israel against the Philistines and defeating Goliath.

4. David became commander over Saul's armies and married Saul's daughter, Michal. He rose in popularity and Saul became jealous.

5. Saul plotted David's death, but David was warned by Saul's son, Jonathan, and fled into the desert. It was during this time in the wilderness that David penned many of the Psalms.

6. Both Saul and Jonathan were killed in battle against the Philistines, and David returned to be crowned as king of Judah.

7. The second half of David's life was marked by tragedy after he committed adultery with Bathsheba, had her husband killed, and was rebuked by the prophet Nathan. As a consequence of his actions, the first child born to David and Bathsheba died.

8. Bathsheba's second son to David would be Solomon. Solomon became the next king and was reputed for his wisdom, wealth, and power. Solomon also wrote Proverbs, Ecclesiastes, and Song of Solomon.

C. Who is David in God's plan?

1. David revealed God's character and plans for Israel.

   a. The story of David is part of a larger story that begins in Genesis and recounts the history of Israel. As Israel developed into a nation and established its identity, it continually chose an identity apart from God. Israel chose an earthly king as its ruler (a symbolic rejection of God and His sovereignty), so God used David to display His character and plans.

   b. "Thus Saul, designated by God at the people's insistence, must be rejected in favor of David, the one whom God chose freely."[1]

2. David's life ultimately pointed to Jesus Christ.

   a. During David's reign, God made a covenant with him, promising that He would establish the house of David eternally: "Your throne shall be established forever" (2 Samuel 7:16).

   b. This covenant was fulfilled through Christ, who is referred to as the "Son of David" (Luke 18:39), "the root of David" (Revelation 5:5), and "the Offspring of David" (Revelation 22:16 NIV).

   c. David is an ancestor of Jesus Christ through both Mary and Joseph.

Summary: Scripture paints for us a picture of a complex man who was heroic and merciful yet "adept at clothing his power-seeking and self-interest in the rhetoric of piety and morality."[2] It is clear from David's actions, however, that he was not chosen because of his inherent goodness. David was chosen because of God's goodness. God is able to use anyone redemptively that He so chooses.

David's Psalms: Where Did They Come From? What Are They?

General Info

:: The word *psalms* is derived from the Greek word *psalmos*, which is translated from the Hebrew *mizmor*. *Mizmor* "signifies music accompanied by stringed instruments."[3]

:: The word *psalm* later came to mean a "song of praise." In the Hebrew Bible, the title of the book of Psalms is *seper t'hillim*, which means "Book of Praises," referring to their content rather than their form.[4]

:: The Psalms are the largest collection of ancient lyric poetry in existence. Lyric poetry "directly expresses the individual emotions of the poet."[5]

:: "They reveal all the religious feelings of the faithful—fears, doubts, and tragedies, as well as triumphs, joys, and hopes."[6]

:: The Psalms formed the "hymnal" of the temple, which is why they often celebrate ordinances of the sanctuary.

:: Types of psalms: lament, thanksgiving, and descriptive praise.

David's Psalms

:: Seventy-three of the psalms are credited to David.

:: David was a musician. Scripture tells us David was a singer of songs and the primary organizer of musical guilds for the sanctuary (1 Chronicles 15:3–28; 16:4–43; 23:1–5; 2 Samuel 6:5). He famously soothed King Saul with his music (1 Samuel 16:17–23).

:: The Psalms were forged amidst David's varying life circumstances. Consistent with the lyric poetry genre, the psalms express the deep emotions of David. They are often raw and angry, but they are also honest and faithful.

:: Walter Brueggemann says: "The Psalms transmit to us ways of speaking that are appropriate to the extremities of human experience."[7]

1 Bruce M. Metzger and Michael D. Coogan, eds., *The Oxford Guide to People & Places of the Bible* (Oxford: Oxford University Press, 2001), 53.
2 Ibid., 52.
3 Allen P. Ross, "Psalms," *The Bible Knowledge Commentary: Old Testament*, ed. John F. Walvoord and Roy B. Zuck, (Colorado Springs: Cook Communications Ministries, 2004), 779.
4 Ibid.
5 Ibid.
6 Ibid.
7 Walter Brueggemann, *The Psalms and the Life of Faith* (Minneapolis:Fortress Press, 1995), 27.

getting started :: chase

After chasing everything the world has to offer,
nothing is more satisfying than God.

What Do We Chase?

Tell me how to please God.

There are days my mind and heart race anxiously at the thought I may be terribly off track in that sincere pursuit. Most days I want to please God. I believe He is real and I believe a day is coming when I will face Him. I want, more than any other thing, for that day to go rather spectacularly. I don't want to be shocked when I am looking into the face of the God of the universe to find I actually missed the point.

One of the great fears of my life is that I would get to the end of my life and realize I lived for the wrong things.

But there are also the days I forget that all the invisible stuff is real, and pleasing God is far from my thoughts and I just chase whatever I want, whatever seems to feel right in the moment. I seek happiness through friends or food or my kids or the approval of people or wasting minutes on Facebook or catching up on shows on Hulu. There are unending distractions to chase.

And then there are the days when I am not chasing meaningless distractions, I am flat-out running from God, arms full of sin.

This study is a story about our God using a man who not only questioned Him but also sinned so atrociously most present-day Christians would avoid him. Yet David at the same time unmistakably possessed the favor of God and chased after His heart in a way that pleased Him. We are going to discover why God's favor rested on a sinful man.

David was not remarkable apart from God. God moved around him and through him in the most powerful stories. But something about the way David saw God transformed the way he lived. He saw God differently than everyone else around him. He loved God and he lived like he loved God. We are going to study the qualities David possessed as a result of what he believed about his God.

What Pleases the Heart of God?

David began as a shepherd boy and became a king. God chose him, the youngest of his brothers, to be the king of Israel, and ultimately His eternal kingdom was realized through David's lineage in the birth of Jesus Christ.

We observe that David dealt more intimately with God, the Father, than any other person did in Scripture, except for Jesus Christ. David's personal prayers were recorded in the Psalms, and in them we get to see a relationship between a sinful man and a perfect God.

What Is the Heart?

As Samuel is about to choose David as the next king, God reminds Samuel, "For the LORD sees not as man sees: man looks on the outward appearance, but the LORD looks on the **heart**" (1 Samuel 16:7, emphasis added). Throughout Scripture God seems to care more about the state of this unseen place in us, our hearts, rather than what everybody else can see in our behavior. While we judge each other by what we can see, God looks deep inside of us to see what nobody else sees. This is the place in us that holds what we love most . . . what we crave . . . what motivates us. This is the place that actually defines who we are.

Whether we acknowledge it or not, our lives are motivated by our hearts. So what we love determines how we live.

Honest

My son, Conner, came home from fifth grade one day and told me his teacher was teaching him to pray like David. Curious what that meant, I asked, "How did David pray?" Conner said, "David didn't tell God what God wanted to hear, he told God what he was really feeling."

Today let's start there. Let's honestly bring our hearts to God and to each other. If any of you are like me, most of the time I don't have any idea how the deepest parts of me are doing. So just take a minute and pray before you move ahead. Ask God to give you insight to narrow down how you are doing right now.

Project

Take a few minutes alone before God and answer these questions. Then come back together and discuss.

When your heart moves fast, what are you excited about?

When you feel disappointed or sad, what is it usually about?

When you feel content and most happy, what is it usually about?

What are the things you think about most?

For God to be pleased with you, what do you think you should be chasing?

Describe God. Answer as if He is one of your friends and you are telling someone about Him.

What is your heart chasing most?

Don't leave this first week with fear or guilt; we just need a starting place, enough honesty and self-awareness to know where we are beginning. If today you are just realizing your heart may be off-track, remember that God has known it well before today. And He is deeply pleased if you recognize it too.

The LORD is near to all who call on him, to all who call on him in truth.

psalm 145:18

I pray these weeks would redefine the way you view God. I pray this time draws you into the most passionate relationship with your Creator. He is so ready to engage our souls.

notes

identity :: 1

The identity we are all chasing has already been given to us by God.

What Is Identity?

Identity is found in the distinct characteristics that set us apart or give us worth.

We want to matter and to make a mark on the world. It feels selfish, even arrogant, to admit it. But every one of us has this need for a significant identity. This need possibly lies at the root of every human interaction and achievement. We all need to know why our life counts and what sets us apart, since life is short and there are a lot of us on this planet.

In the space below describe yourself. Who are you? What do you do? What is your personality like?

Feet Down

I was innocently sitting in science class my sophomore year of high school, waiting for class to start, when two guys known for bullying turned around and decided it was the day to make me their target. I don't remember what they said, but I still can picture where I was sitting and what I was feeling. I felt like I was spinning and could not put my feet down. I could not land on what was true. As they laughed about who they perceived me to be, all I could think was,

"Who am I?"

I knew they did not know me and what they were saying was careless and untrue, but I did not know me and I did not know what was true. It wasn't long after that experience that I met God. And it wasn't until He began to undo me and define me that I finally could put my feet down and stop spinning. But even now, there are still plenty of days I spin, even with God in me.

No matter our age, we often find ourselves with feelings like those I had in high school. We have an identity crisis because we build our identity on things that move—things that aren't dependable or constant.

The list of what we build our identity on goes on and on:

family / bank accounts / friends / personality comfort / house / marriage / leadership / job vacations / children's success / relationships future / abilities / clothes / acceptance / love respect / morals / church / behavior / purpose

David lived a life unconcerned with appearances and image, rooted in a secure identity. Yet those of us who have put our faith in Christ live with the same identity; we just forget.

Let's begin this journey to discover where David's confidence and worth was rooted.

study ::

read 1 samuel 16:1-13

Even though very little is said about David's life directly in these verses, note some of the things we learn

about his life . . .

about his relationship to his father and brothers . . .

about where and how he likely spends his time . . .

about his heart . . .

about his new identity . . .

"And the Spirit of the Lord rushed upon David from that day forward" (1 Samuel 16:13, emphasis added). This single fact would go on to define every moment of the rest of this man's life, every psalm he would write and every obstacle he would overcome. What did it mean for David that the Spirit of God was on him?

Read these verses and consider how those of us who know Christ have a calling similar to David's.

In him we have obtained an inheritance, having been predestined according to the purpose of him who works all things according to the counsel of his will, so that we who were the first to hope in Christ might be to the praise of his glory. In him you also, when you heard the word of truth, the gospel of your salvation, and believed in him, were sealed with the promised Holy Spirit, who is the guarantee of our inheritance until we acquire possession of it, to the praise of his glory.

ephesians 1:11–14

What does He say you are?

What does that mean to you?

But you are a chosen race, a royal priesthood, a holy nation, a people for his own possession, that you may proclaim the excellencies of him who called you out of darkness into his marvelous light. Once you were not a people, but now you are God's people; once you had not received mercy, but now you have received mercy.

1 peter 2:9–10

What does He say you are?

What does that mean to you?

Defining Myself

As long as we try to find our significance and worth in ourselves, we will feel disappointed. Self-esteem only works if we have a self worth esteeming. I am so sinful and selfish that I don't want to put my hope in myself.

Understanding these two truths keeps me from building my hope in myself:

1. We are all lost and pretty messed up, and

2. God in His grace rescued us.

As long as I am looking into myself for my identity, I will either be self-righteous about how great I am, which would be inaccurate, or distraught by the reality of the wreck I actually am.

The gospel steals all self-esteem:

For I know that nothing good dwells in me, that is, in my flesh.

romans 7:18

Defined by God

"Nothing good" dwells in us. This statement in Romans is depressing if you don't hear the rest of the gospel. The whole story, the truth of the gospel, is we get something infinitely more sturdy and fulfilling than self-esteem. For those of us who know Christ, we stand on the unchanging reality that we have been so loved by our God that He purchased us with the blood of His Son. See, we have worth, but it doesn't come from within us—it comes to us from the One who made us. We share in a destiny and the calling David received that day. We have been rushed by the Spirit of God too. We will rule as sons and daughters of God someday. We have an insane calling, an insane identity.

How great is the love the Father has lavished on us, that we should be called children of God! And that is what we are!

1 john 3:1 NIV

If our true worth and significance and identity come from something so solid and eternal as God Himself, we don't have to pretend when we are imperfect. We don't stand on our accomplishments and personality and performance. We stand securely on the nature of an infinite, loving God. We don't have to manage our image or pretend we are okay, when we are really broken and imperfect. The grace God gives us in defining who we are changes everything.

Uniquely Broken

But we have this treasure in jars of clay, to show that the surpassing power belongs to God and not to us.

2 corinthians 4:7

Christ's Spirit is this treasure inside of our broken lives, in us, moving and working in powerful and unique ways. Imperfect jars of clay each shaped uniquely to hold the Spirit of God for different purposes, each with unique marks and cracks and broken places. And through those spaces God shines out. The shameful places are torn down and become the places that are most useful to God.

The gospel strips us down to nothing but builds our hope in a secure, reckless, passionate God who loves us and saved us in spite of our messed-up selves. And then He uses those wrecked places to show His glory.

He is that good and, yes, we are that bad. All of us . . . especially those of us who think we aren't.

Our value comes from God; it can never be found in how we measure up. So whether you feel worthy or ashamed, this news should probably undo you. It is the character of God that gives us worth, not anything we have done or will do.

For by grace you have been saved through faith. And this is not your own doing; it is the gift of God, not a result of works, so that no one may boast.

ephesians 2:8–9

There is freedom in accepting our unworthiness and receiving God's worth. But self-esteem dies hard, especially for those of us who stand on a great performance.

The work of Christ steals all shame but it also steals all of our pride.

Respond

The years David spent in the hills tending sheep birthed a familiar psalm that has comforted every generation since. As you read the psalm, respond to the Lord through the two questions on the next page.

psalm 23

The LORD is my shepherd; I shall not want.
>He makes me lie down in green pastures.

He leads me beside still waters.
>He restores my soul.

He leads me in paths of righteousness
>for his name's sake.

Even though I walk through the valley of the shadow of death,
>I will fear no evil,

for you are with me;
>your rod and your staff,

>they comfort me.

You prepare a table before me
>in the presence of my enemies;

you anoint my head with oil;
>my cup overflows.

Surely goodness and mercy shall follow me
>all the days of my life,

and I shall dwell in the house of the LORD forever.

study &

Who are you, Lord?   What do you want for me?

God desires for you to know His heart. He wants to lead you beside still waters and to restore your soul. He wants you to embrace your identity as His child. These are my hopes and prayers for you this week as you take time to reflect on His Word through these projects.

be.

Be still, and know that I am God. I will be exalted among the nations, I will be exalted in the earth!

psalm 46:10

It is hard to make the time and the space and to make our worlds quiet. We have to fight for it. It was in the quiet of the hills that an intimate relationship between David and God was born. It was when David was alone.

Get alone with God, with no agenda. Go outside and sit; turn off your phone. Pray and be with God. Confess your dependence. Thank Him. And listen.

> I lift up my eyes to the hills.
>   From where does my help come?
> My help comes from the LORD,
> who made heaven and earth.

psalm 121:1–2

So then you are no longer strangers and aliens, but you are fellow citizens with the saints and members of the household of God, built on the foundation of the apostles and prophets, Christ Jesus himself being the cornerstone.

ephesians 2:19–20

consider.

These blocks represent the things you have used to construct your identity. What have you built your identity around? On each block write something you have used to define yourself. (For example: kids, job, appearance, abilities, friends.)

We all know these things are inadequate. But we are still building our lives and our worth on them.

How do you feel if the things you listed are threatened?

Who are you if you lose all of this?

risk.

How much are you trying to control your image or what others think of you? Answer these questions:

Do you freely confess your current struggles to close friends?

When someone accuses you of something, do you immediately get defensive?

Are you quick to condemn when you hear about someone else screwing up? And do you feel like you are above making massive mistakes?

Do you get frantic when you feel misunderstood?

Do people think you have it all together?

There is freedom in understanding we are all equally and completely messed up, selfish, and prideful. We belittle the God of the universe whether we have an affair or we just worry He won't provide. None of us is above messing up, even in what some might consider small ways. We all have sinned and fallen short of God's glory. There is no way anyone can live as though they are better than someone else. God is our only hope, our Defender, our Definition, our Righteousness. Apart from Him there is no good thing.

wrestle.

As we begin this journey, chasing the heart of God together, wrestle with what you know about God. Write a letter to Him—describe how you feel about Him right now. How do you feel when you approach Him to pray? How do you think He views you? Is His definition of you hard to believe?

Be honest. Put words to how you view Him and how you think He views you.

Dear God,

Conclusion

The right answer is to rest our identity in the God who created us and defines us. He gives us our identity. The right answer sounds amazing and even potentially fulfilling. But most days it feels impossible to believe in an invisible kingdom, in an invisible God who actually loves us. So we attach ourselves and our worth to things we can see. We try to control our image, since what is inside feels impossible to fix.

This is the war that often consumes our lives; here lies the root of insecurity. But also on a good day when we feel our image is intact, there lies the root of pride. And neither insecurity nor pride serves as a fulfilling basis for our identity.

These questions matter, since they lie at the core of our hearts and navigate our lives.

Who am I?

How am I finding my identity in things outside of God? Is it working?

How do I align my identity around God's character?

Do you want to know why David lived so confidently, so boldly? He actually believed this stuff. David believed God is who He says He is and what God said about him was true. David's God was real. David was God's and David knew it.

courage :: 2

The fear of God makes people brave.

For God gave us a spirit not of fear but of power and love and self-control.

2 timothy 1:7

Seeing God

Fear has so captivated our minds we don't even recognize it anymore. It's just how we think. We live paralyzed, afraid to stand out yet also afraid of being invisible, afraid of something terrible happening yet also afraid something good will never happen. We live afraid of people and we think all of these thoughts are normal. We don't live seeing God, we live seeing worst-case scenarios.

While everyone stood around acting like they believed in God, David actually was experiencing Him. This is why God worked so powerfully through David's life. God was a matter of fact to David. God was so real, David found everyone else silly when they stood around not doing anything because they were afraid. He was recklessly brave simply because he knew God was real and with him.

Do we just confess an intellectual belief in God or is He real enough to impact our circumstances? Do we see God rather than physical realities? Fear is not just a little thing. Fear is stopping us from the things we are meant to be doing, the things God means for us to accomplish. And we must begin to experience God and hear Him or we will just stand there looking at whatever giants we face, unable to move forward. We need courage. But courage feels impossible to muster up on days we feel paralyzed by fear.

David wasn't especially courageous when he faced a giant; he just believed God was bigger than the man he faced. He believed God was real and with him. The same God with David is with us. God actually has plans for our days, and seeing God gives me the courage I need to live out His plans, no matter the risk.

> For this people's heart has grown dull,
>   and with their ears they can barely hear,
>   and their eyes they have closed;
> lest they should **see with their eyes**
>   and **hear with their ears**
> and **understand with their heart**
> and turn, and I would heal them.
>
> acts 28:27, emphasis added

Do we see and hear God? Would we live in fear if we did?

Our fear of God has to expand to be greater than our fear of anything else. Fearing God simply means that, above any other thing, we love and want to please Him. The first of the Ten Commandments is, "You shall have no other gods before me" (Exodus 20:3). When God is in His right place, He will be the only thing we fear, the only thing we worship.

Be willing to go out on a limb with Me. If that is where I am leading you, it is the safest place to be. . . . Your desire to live close to Me is at odds with your attempts to minimize risk. You are approaching a crossroads in your journey. In order to follow Me wholeheartedly, you must relinquish your tendency to play it safe.

Let Me lead you step by step through this day. If your primary focus is on Me, you can walk along perilous paths without being afraid. Eventually, you will learn to relax and enjoy the adventure of our journey together. As long as you stay close to Me, My sovereign Presence protects you wherever you go.

sarah young, *Jesus Calling*[8]

8 Sarah Young, *Jesus Calling: Enjoying Peace in His Presence* (Nashville: Thomas Nelson, 2004), 360.

study ::

read 1 samuel 17:1-51

What did the Israelite army believe about the situation, and how did they act upon their beliefs?

What was on the line if they fought?

What did David believe about the situation, and how did he act upon his beliefs?

How was David different from every other man there? What gave him the courage to act?

What was David's motive for fighting Goliath? What did he want most?

Nothing to Lose

The smaller this life gets and the bigger God and the next life get, the more we are willing to risk here on this earth. We live courageously because in light of God's glory, we don't have as much to lose. Courage is grounded in a big view of God.

A truly dangerous person is one who has nothing to lose. Saul and all of the Israelite men were protective of themselves, their freedom, their comfortable lives. David did not see what he might lose, he saw God; he saw God's glory and name being mocked, and in faith he was motivated to bring glory to God. David did not live protectively of this life; he had nothing to lose here, because he believed his God was real and heaven was coming.

Fear is rooted in unbelief and unbelief is sin. Courage is fundamentally a fight for faith. We fight to believe all the way down to the deepest parts of us that God is real and enough. He alone makes us brave.

Romans 8

For all who are led by the Spirit of God are sons of God. For you did not receive the spirit of slavery to fall back into fear, but you have received the Spirit of adoption as sons, by whom we cry, "Abba! Father!"

romans 8:14–15

Why does Romans say we don't have to fall back into fear?

How does God being your loving Father inspire courage?

Courage in the Everyday

One who is faithful in a very little is also faithful in much.

luke 16:10a

Courage is grown in the mundane, small pieces of our lives.

So what does it look like to bravely follow God in the small things?
:: Ask the cashier how she is and listen as she responds.

:: Deal with unresolved conflicts at work, in your family, with your friends.

:: Make friends at the park or in your dorm or at your office.

:: Forgive the friend who keeps hurting you.

:: Serve your church in a way no one sees.

:: Be intentional with time you have with your kids or your friends. Be present.

:: Make the most of every opportunity to respond to need, whether it is the homeless man on the side of the road or your grandparents who need a visit.

Every day wake up and live fully for God's glory. These are some suggestions, but where is God calling you to live more bravely in the everyday?

Courage in the Impossible

Something about our position as God's children should eradicate our fear. We should not live in a paralyzed state, because there is power in understanding our Father, God. He is enough and He sees us. So whether our Goliath is a move overseas to serve unreached people or facing a new diagnosis of cancer, God is with us and He will not forsake us.

Last night I sat in my car with a dear friend whose husband recently moved out. She is the mother of four young kids. Fear flooded the car as we sat considering her future.

There are never words in moments like this. I grabbed her arms and said, "God sees you. He sees your kids. He is real and alive and pressing into this, even though it feels like He turned His head for a moment. He didn't turn His head. He is here." Then we talked to Him. There in the driveway, outside of little bedrooms with little hurting people and big unknown futures, we talked to an invisible God.

And in that moment we remembered that He was real and coming and that today He would be enough to face the scariest things. We don't face this life alone. He is behind us in all things. Do we see Him?

When David was a child, tending his sheep and obeying God, when no one saw him in the fields, he was building a story of faith. When the time came for him to face his giant, David feared God on that impossible day because he had learned to fear God in the everyday. Courage for the impossible is most often built by God growing our faith in Him in the everyday. We live by faith, not by sight.

Respond

Work through the psalm and consider what David believed his God could do. In what areas do you need to expand what you believe your God can do? As you read the psalm below, respond to God through the questions on the next page.

psalm 27

> The LORD is my light and my salvation;
> whom shall I fear?
> The LORD is the stronghold of my life;
> of whom shall I be afraid?
> When evildoers assail me
> to eat up my flesh,
> my adversaries and foes,
> it is they who stumble and fall.
> Though an army encamp against me,
> my heart shall not fear;
> though war arise against me,
> yet I will be confident.
> One thing have I asked of the LORD,
> that will I seek after:
> that I may dwell in the house of the LORD
> all the days of my life,
> to gaze upon the beauty of the LORD
> and to inquire in his temple.
> For he will hide me in his shelter
> in the day of trouble;

he will conceal me under the cover of his tent;
     he will lift me high upon a rock.
And now my head shall be lifted up
     above my enemies all around me,
and I will offer in his tent
     sacrifices with shouts of joy;
I will sing and make melody to the Lord.
     Hear, O Lord, when I cry aloud;
be gracious to me and answer me!
You have said, "Seek my face."
My heart says to you,
     "Your face, Lord, do I seek."
     Hide not your face from me.
Turn not your servant away in anger,
     O you who have been my help.
Cast me not off; forsake me not,
     O God of my salvation!
     For my father and my mother have forsaken me,
     but the Lord will take me in.
Teach me your way, O Lord,
     and lead me on a level path
     because of my enemies.
Give me not up to the will of my adversaries;
     for false witnesses have risen against me,
     and they breathe out violence.
I believe that I shall look upon the goodness of the Lord
     in the land of the living!
     Wait for the Lord;
be strong, and let your heart take courage;
     wait for the Lord!

Who are you, Lord?  What do you want for me?

As you approach your time with God this week, pray He will expose the strongholds that keep you from recklessly following Him.

consider.

Consider these three verses before answering the questions that follow:

Then Samuel took the horn of oil and anointed him in the midst of his brothers. And the Spirit of the LORD rushed upon David from that day forward. And Samuel rose up and went to Ramah.

1 samuel 16:13

For God gave us a spirit not of fear but of power and love and self-control.

2 timothy 1:7

But you will receive power when the Holy Spirit has come upon you, and you will be my witnesses in Jerusalem and in all Judea and Samaria, and to the end of the earth.

acts 1:8

Compare the power given to David with the power given to those who believe in Christ.

Why do we limit the Holy Spirit's voice and power in our lives?

Since we have the same spirit of faith according to what has been written, "I believed, and so I spoke," we also believe, and so we also speak.

2 corinthians 4:13

ask.

Pray and ask God what He is calling you to do, to say, or to be that you have not previously considered because of fear or a hard heart.

Write down the things that are brought to mind or pressed on your heart.

_____

_____

_____

_____

_____

_____

_____

For this people's heart has grown dull, and with their ears they can barely hear, and their eyes they have closed.

acts 28:27a

imagine.

Imagine what it would look like if you lived out a childlike, reckless, and courageous faith like David had in 1 Samuel 17. Draw what comes to mind.

What is keeping you from living out that kind of faith?

Who or what is your "Goliath"?

Who or what causes you to feel insecurity and doubt as David's brother did in 1 Samuel 17:28?

commit.

Write your own psalm (prayer) and consider including some of these things:

:: Describe and praise God for who you know Him to be.

:: Ask for forgiveness for not hearing or seeing the call and power of God.

:: Confess ways you have not believed God.

:: Commit to obeying God in the ways He is calling you to walk courageously.

Conclusion

What if we became insanely courageous and began to live the stories God has written for us?

What if we could truly love people without fear of how they would receive us?

What if we could give without needing anything in return?

What if we actually began living our dreams instead of squashing them back into safer places?

I believe God is calling us to a life like this, but not in our own strength. He wants us to see that He is able. He is for us. He is our hope and we live this out for His glory. We were made for that. We were made to display the glory of our Creator through our lives, through our freedom from fear. Fearing and loving God alone makes every other fear disappear.

notes

obedience :: 3

The more we trust God, the more we obey Him.

For you bless the righteous, O LORD;
you cover him with favor as with a shield.

psalm 5:12

Teenage Rebellion

I remember the sound my heart made. It was pounding so hard, so loud, fighting against my efforts to stay calm, I thought it may win and beat me down. Sitting on the floor of our room in the sorority house with my best friend, Kathryn, we had been praying and both of us couldn't shake the feeling we needed to pray for our friend Sarah. So we did. Sarah may have been the most confident and admired girl in our sorority, and after we finished praying we knew we were supposed to talk to her about God. I had known Sarah since middle school and never once talked to her about God. But I was learning to trust the leadings God was putting in me. Still, as Kathryn and I headed down the stairs to find her, I couldn't help whispering to myself, "I hope she is not here," and "God, I'll obey, but you'd better show up."

When Sarah got to her room, Kathryn and I were waiting for her and, certain we were about to look so foolish, we awkwardly told her we had been praying and now we were going to tell her about God. I kind-of butchered the whole thing. But immediately she started crying, and she sat down on our floor without a moment's hesitation and eagerly waited to hear what we had to say. It may have been one of the most beautiful things I have ever seen. Sarah was hurting for God and God sent us awkwardly to get her.

It was one time I obeyed the odd and small leading of God. How many other times I have not and how many beautiful moments I'm sure I have missed.

Most of my life something rebellious has risen up in me when I hear the word *obey*. I'd turn into a toddler, or maybe more like a teenager, who knows what is right and just doesn't want to do it. I learned as a child that my behavior mattered more than my heart. My parents were certainly not the only culprits for teaching me this; school, church, friends, and jobs all taught me this. So naturally the feelings of pressure that accompany such an upbringing make me cringe when I hear words like *obey* or *submit*. And naturally all of that eventually carried over to my relationship with God.

However, God began to transform my view of Him in college, and as my view of Him grew, my trust in Him grew and my obedience to Him grew, not out of fear but because I wanted Him more than my own way. I wanted Him more than my friends' approval. So on nights spent on floors, praying, when He told me to do awkward, foolish things, I actually did them.

When I read the stories you are going to read below, I am convicted, and I desperately want to be like David, not Saul. Saul was the king prior to David, but he lost God's blessing on the day described in these verses. It was not because of his behavior; it was because of his heart. This is a key point because, as we will see later in this study, some of the sin David will commit is heinous too. So if the issue is not that Saul sinned more than David, what, then, is the issue?

Compare David's and Saul's hearts in these two similar battles. What were the differences in these two men?

study ::
saul

read 1 samuel 15:1–31

What did God ask of Saul?

How did Saul disobey?

What motivated Saul to disobey?

What was God's response?

What was it about Saul's heart that displeased God?

study ::
david

read 1 samuel 23:2-14

What did God ask of David?

How did David respond?

What do you think motivated David to obey?

What was God's response?

What was it about David's heart that pleased God?

Look at these two lists of motivations that drove Saul and David. Think about your life and what motives are driving you.

Saul	David	Your Motivations
Practical wisdom	Reckless obedience	
People's approval	God's opinion	
Self-provision	God's provision	
Recognition	God's approval	
Immediate reward	Other people's welfare	
Power	Dependence	
Self-protection	God's protection	

David trusted God. He trusted God's character, unlike Saul and
unlike Adam and Eve. Adam and Eve disobeyed because they
thought God was holding out on them. They did not trust God.
Trust in the character of God is foundational to obedience.

Following the Rules

Many of us hear the word *obedience* and based on past experiences we feel pressure, and words like *rules*, *punishment*, and *shame* come to mind. Deep in the crevasses of present-day Christendom lies the backward theology that good behavior pleases God. But morality—doing good things for the sake of doing good things—has never won God's favor. As we'll see later, David's life was far from moral. David became tangled in adultery and even murder. He was not moral, yet he was considered right before God.

It's not that Saul sinned more than David. So why was Saul rejected by God and David accepted? Something about the invisible places within each of the men was fundamentally different toward God.

We know that a person is not justified by works of the law but through faith in Jesus Christ, so we also have believed in Christ Jesus, in order to be justified by faith in Christ and not by works of the law, because by works of the law no one will be justified.

galatians 2:16

Morality is something we achieve, while righteousness is something we receive. God makes us right because of Jesus, and our love and obedience to Him is empowered and accomplished through Christ.

As good and miraculous as this is, our pride doesn't want it to be true. We want to be good enough on our own.

Faith in God has always been and will always be what makes us right before God.

Faith = Righteousness that comes from Christ = God's acceptance

---

For it is by grace you have been saved, through faith—and this is not from yourselves . . .

ephesians 2:8 NIV

Belittling God

At some point Saul quit trusting God. He started caring more about pleasing the people around him than obeying God, and he did not see his sin as a big deal. I am constantly guilty of the same thing. The sins I can hide become acceptable and so I accept them. I tuck them back where no one sees and I let them grow. Then I am surprised when I feel sick from chasing everything I knew would make my insides hurt. The reality is I would rather have a day full of all my favorite things than a moment of tasting God. I belittle God and the offense is so great because I offend Someone so great.

We all lack faith and belittle God regularly. We are no better than Saul; we are pleasing men instead of God. But do we really see how sinful we are before our good and holy God?

John Piper says the mark of a believer is not the absence of sin but the fact that we are fighting sin.[9] We should feel uncomfortable with our sin because it offends our God. But when confronted with his sin, Saul did not repent, he begged God to save his reputation. Saul's relationship with his people was more important to him than his relationship with God, and he justified his sinful actions by claiming he had good intentions.

Most of us, if we are honest, have been there. Like Saul, we sin against God but explain our reasons so beautifully that everyone but God pats us on the back. Or in some cases, we might avoid sin at all costs, but our lack of sin is motivated by what others think of us; it has little or nothing to do with God.

God simply asks us for our obedience and our trust. What was so beautiful and unique about David was his deep affection for God and his desire to obey Him no matter what it meant for his time on earth and no matter what anyone else thought.

9   John Piper, *Future Grace* (Colorado Springs: Multnomah, 2005), 329.

Respond

Look at this psalm David wrote while running from Saul. What is it about David's heart that so pleased God?

Psalm 63

O God, you are my God; earnestly I seek you;
  my soul thirsts for you;
my flesh faints for you,
  as in a dry and weary land where there is no water.
So I have looked upon you in the sanctuary,
  beholding your power and glory.
Because your steadfast love is better than life,
  my lips will praise you.
So I will bless you as long as I live;
  in your name I will lift up my hands.
My soul will be satisfied as with fat and rich food,
  and my mouth will praise you with joyful lips,
when I remember you upon my bed,
  and meditate on you in the watches of the night;
for you have been my help,
  and in the shadow of your wings I will sing for joy.
My soul clings to you;
  your right hand upholds me.
But those who seek to destroy my life
  shall go down into the depths of the earth;
they shall be given over to the power of the sword;
  they shall be a portion for jackals.
But the king shall rejoice in God;
  all who swear by him shall exult,
  for the mouths of liars will be stopped.

Who are you, Lord?   &   What do you want for me?

Why is it difficult for us to obey? My hope for you as you approach these projects is that you will identify some of the things keeping you from experiencing the blessing of obedience.

reflect.

Look at your own heart in light of Saul's.

Saul said to Samuel, "I have sinned, for I have transgressed the commandment of the LORD and your words, because I feared the people and obeyed their voice."

1 samuel 15:24

Has your fear of people become greater than your fear of God?

If yes, give some examples.

Respond to God about this struggle in your life.

compare.

Check out these verses:

> For you will not delight in sacrifice, or I would give it;
>> you will not be pleased with a burnt offering.
> The sacrifices of God are a broken spirit;
>> a broken and contrite heart, O God, you will not despise.

psalm 51:16-17

For in it the righteousness of God is revealed from faith for faith, as it is written, "The righteous shall live by faith."

romans 1:17

And he believed the LORD, and he counted it to him as righteousness.

genesis 15:6

And without faith it is impossible to please him, for whoever would draw near to God must believe that he exists and that he rewards those who seek him.

hebrews 11:6

---

project :: 2

What do you believe is the difference between morality and true righteousness? Write the qualities of each below. List the different qualities between morality and true righteousness.

Morality

_____

_____

_____

_____

_____

_____

_____

_____

True Righteousness

_____

_____

_____

_____

_____

_____

_____

_____

On most days what do you feel like it is God wants from you?

What do you think He actually wants from you?

rewind.

And because you are sons, God has sent the Spirit of his Son into our hearts, crying, "Abba! Father!"

galatians 4:6

Oftentimes our view of obedience and even our view of God come from our relationship with our earthly father. Explore how this earthly relationship is affecting your relationship with God.

If you had a father in your life growing up, write about what he expected from you as a child.

Did you measure up to those expectations?

How has that impacted the way you relate to God?

imagine.

If God were your physical Father on earth, describe what kind of Father you think He would be.

What would He do with you?

What would He hope for you?

What would He expect from you?

What would your conversations be about?

Conclusion

There are so many reasons we cringe when we hear words like *obedience* and *submission*:

:: We don't believe God asks us to obey for our own good.

:: We don't believe God truly cares for us.

:: We don't believe God knows everything.

:: We want to be our own captains.

:: We want to control our own lives.

I am a parent now and I see all of these same struggles in my kids. Learning to trust God is a lot like a child learning to trust a father. It takes time and a genuine relationship.

Do you trust that God's desires for you are good?

Do you think you control your life better than He does?

Relationships are always built on trust and trust leads to obedience.

notes

belief :: 4

*How we live every second of every day will flow
out of what we believe about God.*

Promise Me

Recently, my good friend Amanda pulled together a room full of neighbors to do a Bible study. Most of the room wasn't sure what they believed about God. I was given a few minutes to teach about God and grace, and when I did, Colleen, who sat closest to me, stopped me and said, "I find it hard to believe we don't have to do anything to measure up to God. It sounds good, but I just can't believe that."

I sometimes doubt too. Every once in a while the thought will go through my mind,

"What if there is no God?"

Heaven and angels and hell and God in heaven and Christ raised from the dead . . . it's easy to question, and in those moments my soul feels dark. It's as if I've just been yanked out of the most comfortable, beautiful home and I'm left in a dark alley, alone with nothing. In that moment I taste hopelessness.

After the thought passes and I remember the undeniable presence of God everywhere in my life, even in every piece of creation, peace and hope flood me again. If we are honest, there are moments or seasons we all doubt, because every foundational thing about us depends on invisible stuff.

I stand on the promise that I will live for eternity as a child of God (Romans 8:15), that God will work all things together for good because I love Him (Romans 8:28), and that He lives in me and is a very present help in struggles (Psalm 46:1). I trust He prepared good works for me to do in advance and I just have to look to Him and He will carry them out (Ephesians 2:10). I stand on the promise that He formed me in my mother's womb and knows my every thought (Psalm 139:13).

These promises are so deep within me, they are holding me up and driving me. These promises are made even more beautiful because they are not hinging on some spectacular performance from me while I am here on earth. God promises these things and I am just a recipient. But do we really believe all of this invisible stuff?

How often do we doubt God in some form or fashion?

Daily.

Doubt is the root of all sin. I know we all doubt Him, because if we fully believed God every moment, we would all be living radical, completely sold-out lives. I think David's incredible God-filled life was evidence of just that.

Jesus said to him, "Have you believed because you have seen me? Blessed are those who have not seen and yet have believed."

john 20:29

God promised David things that would lay the foundation for all of the promises we stand on today.

study ::

read 2 samuel 7:1-17

(Note: These verses point to Jesus, but verse 14 is talking about Solomon.)

What is the overarching promise God made to David?

Fulfilled Promises

This enormous promise of an eternal kingdom that God makes to David is a beautiful promise and we get to be a part of it through Christ. We are blessed to be on this side of the cross, looking back on the redeeming work of Christ rather than waiting in expectation of it. The hope of the world has always been and always will be Jesus Christ.

And behold, you will conceive in your womb and bear a son, and you shall call his name Jesus. He will be great and will be called the Son of the Most High. And the Lord God will give to him the throne of his father David, and he will reign over the house of Jacob forever, and of his kingdom there will be no end.

luke 1:31–33

I, Jesus, have sent my angel to testify to you about these things for the churches. I am the root and the descendant of David, the bright morning star.

revelation 22:16

Write about how the promises God made to David affect you today.

Read David's response to God's promises.

Then King David went in and sat before the LORD and said, "Who am I, O Lord GOD, and what is my house, that you have brought me thus far? And yet this was a small thing in your eyes, O Lord GOD. . . . And what more can David say to you? For you know your servant, O Lord GOD! . . . Now therefore may it please you to bless the house of your servant, so that it may continue forever before you. For you, O Lord GOD, have spoken, and with your blessing shall the house of your servant be blessed forever."

2 samuel 7:18–19, 20, 29

Put yourself in David's position. How did these promises change his life?

How did these promises change his relationship with God?

And have mercy on those who doubt.

jude 1:22

Questioning

I was eighteen, sitting on the bed of my dorm room reading the cries of David, this mess of a man, in the Psalms. As I read, it was as if God were telling me,

Stop, Jennie. Stop pretending. Stop playing nice.

These words wrecked me and I wondered if I really was safe enough to talk to God this way. But I was tired of pretending. So I got in my car and started driving, playing music loud enough to cover the sounds of my yelling. I yelled at God for the first time in my life. He was supposed to bless me because I was serving Him. And yet I couldn't get the approval I was longing for from friends, from family. I could not reconcile unresolved hurts from my past and I could not understand how God could have allowed those hurts to happen. My life was still not working. I was moral and I thought God owed me something for it. I thought He owed me happiness.

I finished yelling at God. By this point I had driven far out of the city. I came to a pond and I got out and knelt on the ground, and there in the quiet after the first fight I had with God . . .

He was there. He fell into my questions in the most brilliant way I had ever seen or felt before. He fell into the space in me I thought would push Him further away. He fell into the places I had sinned against Him. He met me in my anger and reminded me of His great unwavering love for me. I was His and nothing I felt, no matter how wrong, could shake Him from me. And in that night He was enough for me; His approval felt better than the elusive compliments I had been chasing from people, and in trusting Him with my hurt and disappointment, I found Him in it with me. He didn't feel like my enemy anymore. My God was real and He loved me despite my sense of entitlement, my doubts, and my pride. It is one of my favorite and most intimate moments I have ever had with God.

God can handle our doubts. He is big enough. But we have got to quit pretending faith is easy. We fight for faith and ask God to give it.

And Lord, haste the day when my faith shall be sight,
The clouds be rolled back as a scroll;
The trump shall resound, and the Lord shall descend,
Even so, it is well with my soul.
It is well, with my soul,
It is well, with my soul,
It is well, it is well, with my soul.

horatio spafford, "It Is Well With My Soul"

Respond

As God made a promise in 2 Samuel 7 to David, He was revealing His plan for salvation. Throughout the Psalms David was overwhelmed by the protection and salvation he received from the Lord. We have the same story as David, the promise of participating in a kingdom that lasts forever, because of Christ. Read as David reflects on the covenant God has made with him.

Psalm 110

The LORD says to my Lord:
    "Sit at my right hand,
until I make your enemies your footstool."
The LORD sends forth from Zion
    your mighty scepter.
    Rule in the midst of your enemies!
Your people will offer themselves freely
    on the day of your power,
    in holy garments;
from the womb of the morning,
    the dew of your youth will be yours.
The LORD has sworn
    and will not change his mind,
"You are a priest forever
    after the order of Melchizedek."
The Lord is at your right hand;
    he will shatter kings on the day of his wrath.
He will execute judgment among the nations,
    filling them with corpses;
he will shatter chiefs
    over the wide earth.
He will drink from the brook by the way;
    therefore he will lift up his head.

Who are you, Lord? What do you want for me?

As you spend time with the Lord this week, wrestle through your faith. What is your faith built upon?

wrestle.

Be completely honest. What are the areas of your faith you find yourself doubting most often? Write them in the "Doubts" section below.

Doubts

Scripture

Now look up scripture concerning each doubt you feel and write out God's truth in the "Scripture" section beside each doubt you listed. This Web site may prove helpful in your search: http://www.biblegateway.com/.

Take care, brothers, lest there be in any of you an evil, unbelieving heart, leading you to fall away from the living God.

hebrews 3:12

reflect.

Describe a time in your life when, beyond a shadow of a doubt, God was real to you.

. . . a time when something happened that was beyond coincidence.

. . . a time that gave you confidence that there is an Author to our lives.

The word *remember* is found in Scripture over 150 times.[10] It's not every day in our lives we have a mountaintop experience with God. He wants to assure us our faith is real through our memories of the times when it was undoubtedly real and through the promises of His Word.

But unfortunately we forget. Come back to this page whenever you are having doubts, and remember again the times when He was most real to you.

10 http://www.twopaths.com/faq_wordcount.htm

imagine.

If you met God today, imagine what you would talk about. What would you ask Him?

What would you celebrate with Him?

What would you wish you had done differently?

What would it feel like to see all you have believed become a visible reality?

The day you meet God face-to-face will one day be a reality. Are you living like it will be?

And no longer shall each one teach his neighbor and each his brother, saying, "Know the LORD,"
for they shall all know me, from the least of them to the greatest, declares the LORD. For I will
forgive their iniquity, and I will remember their sin no more.

jeremiah 31:34

commit.

What are the areas in which you continue to doubt God, His provision, or His goodness?

On this side of the line
write the areas you doubt.

On this side of the line
write your prayer to Him,
asking Him for more faith
in these areas.

Note: Sometimes you can't and shouldn't quit wrestling with God. Some doubts need more than a few scriptures to comfort. But you can commit to dealing with your doubt through counseling, personal study, and prayer. Just don't walk away from studying this week until you have a plan to hash these things out with God.

Conclusion

I think of my kids and how right answers on their lips do not move me, the perfectly combed hair and put-together table manners do not move me. But my child looking at me, confused about the evil and suffering he just observed, or my child wondering why she did not make it when she did her absolute best, or my child crying as I have to punish him and it just hurts . . . then I am moved—moved to hold, to love, to restore, to comfort, to be.

So often as believers we are afraid to question God.

Question. And don't apologize.

As if He can't handle our doubt or questions or hurt or disappointment. As if He wanted happy robots. We are how He made us: weak and needy, confused and complicated and in need of God, especially a God we can't understand.

I need a God whom I cannot understand. I need a God big enough to have purposes for my life that are beyond what I can see. And because He happens to be that big and purposeful, our shallow, small hearts will question.

And that big God will move; He'll move toward me to hold, to love, to restore, to comfort, to be. And I would never want to miss that.

notes

repentance :: 5

It is God's mercy to show us our sin and lead us to repentance.

Hiding or Running

I couldn't find Kate. We were all home after our Easter church service, grandparents and other family seated at the table and ready to eat. I had left Kate in my room after having to punish her. Kate, who was seven years old at the time, rarely gets in trouble; she is a joyful, easy kid. After she had come to understand what she had done wrong and had served her time-out, I expected to find her drying her tears, wiping her nose, and preparing to join us. But she was nowhere to be found. I called loudly for her and even went around the outside of the house once. I came back into my room and heard sniffles coming from my closet. I opened the door and could hear her crying but couldn't see her.

I got on my hands and knees and there she was under all my hanging clothes, arms and legs mixed in with sandals and boots. She was overwhelmed with shame and couldn't face anyone, so she hid. She thought she had lost me; she thought she had forever messed everything up.

Like Kate, we all mess up, even after God has done so much for us. Guilt and shame sink into the holes of our failures and we either run from those feelings or they paralyze us.

But whether we are ignoring our sin or sitting in the junk of it on a closet floor, we all feel shame. Some of us just cope with that feeling better than others. We like to mask our weakness till we find ourselves believing we're all right.

It is trouble to feel broken. It is trouble to need God.

There are two places we typically run when we see our sin.

1. We hide like Adam and Eve, making fig leaves . . . we hide in our closets under clothes of religion or morality.

2. We run from God in outright rebellion like the prodigal son.

Both responses take us further from freedom, further from God's love.

Repentance is the confession of the specific ways I have offended God, turning away from that sin and toward God for forgiveness. God doesn't ask us to confess our sin so we will feel guilty. He asks us to confess our sin to find freedom and to come back to Him.

He who conceals his sins does not prosper, but whoever confesses and renounces them finds mercy.

proverbs 28:13 NIV

David sinned in some big ways, as we are going to study, and when God showed him his sin, he didn't hide and he didn't run. He fell before God. Something about coming to the end of ourselves, when we can't pretend we are good anymore, shows us just how much we always needed God. Seeing our great need for God leads us back to Him.

study ::

read 2 samuel 11

and

2 samuel 12:1-14

What were David's sins?

How did God choose to convict David of his sin?

What was David's response to God after he was convicted?

Those who are well have no need of a physician, but those who are sick. I came not to call the righteous, but sinners.

mark 2:17

But God chose what is foolish in the world to shame the wise; God chose what is weak in the world to shame the strong.

1 corinthians 1:27

But he said to me, "My grace is sufficient for you, for my power is made perfect in weakness." Therefore I will boast all the more gladly of my weaknesses, so that the power of Christ may rest upon me.

2 corinthians 12:9

Use the scales below to think about your own level of conviction.

Do you live in need of God?

1------2------3------4------5------6------7------8------9-----10

I don't live like
I need God

I live in great
need of God

Do you live with an awareness of your sin?

1------2------3------4------5------6------7------8------9-----10

I don't believe
I sin often

I am aware of my
constant sinfulness

study

Do you grieve the ways you have offended God?

1------2------3------4------5------6------7------8------9-----10

I do not grieve my
offenses

I am grieved
by my sin

The goal of repentance is not to air out our junk. The goal and beauty of repentance is that it restores our relationship with God. When we acknowledge our sin, we state what God already knows, and we state that we need Him to make us right. Pride is destroyed with transparent repentance.

David could not stand the sin of a man taking a lamb, while he himself had murdered a man and taken his wife. Wasn't this human of him? We all do this: we see the sin of others so clearly but can't seem to remember how we have offended God.

Repentance is painful because none of us want to admit how far we are from good.

A contrite heart pleases God, a heart that sees its need for a Savior.

> The sacrifices of God are a broken spirit;
> a broken and **contrite** heart, O God, you will not
> despise.

psalm 51:17, emphasis added

God doesn't despise remorseful hearts, because He can work them. On the following pages you are going to glimpse into one of the most brutal, passionate journal entries ever. Our hope to be rescued from our sin is never hope in itself; it is hope in the character of God. God is the One who delivers, restores, and cleans. He alone is able to save.

Respond

This Psalm is an intense glimpse into the heart of this broken man, David. As you read the Psalm, respond to the questions on the next page.

Psalm 32

> Blessed is the one whose transgression is forgiven,
>> whose sin is covered.
> Blessed is the man against whom the LORD counts no iniquity,
>> and in whose spirit there is no deceit.
> For when I kept silent, my bones wasted away
>> through my groaning all day long.
> For day and night your hand was heavy upon me;
>> my strength was dried up as by the heat of summer.

I acknowledged my sin to you,
>and I did not cover my iniquity;

I said, "I will confess my transgressions to the Lord,"
>and you forgave the iniquity of my sin.

Therefore let everyone who is godly
>offer prayer to you at a time when you may be found;

surely in the rush of great waters,
>they shall not reach him.

You are a hiding place for me;
>you preserve me from trouble;
>you surround me with shouts of deliverance.

I will instruct you and teach you in the way you should go;
>I will counsel you with my eye upon you.

Be not like a horse or a mule, without understanding,
>which must be curbed with bit and bridle,
>or it will not stay near you.

Many are the sorrows of the wicked,
>but steadfast love surrounds the one who trusts in the Lord.

Be glad in the Lord, and rejoice, O righteous,
>and shout for joy, all you upright in heart!

Who are you, Lord? & What do you want for me?

As you approach God in study this week, my hope is you will come with a broken and contrite heart. Some of you feel broken to the point of shame. I pray you will find rest in the freedom of God's encompassing grace.

consider.

In what areas do you need to experience God's forgiveness?

Are there any sins you are holding onto that are causing you shame? Name them.

From what we have studied this week, what do you think God would say to you concerning your shame?

To the Lord our God belong mercy and forgiveness, for we have rebelled against him.

daniel 9:9

discover.

God knows our hearts. We are unable to hide from Him. Spend some time alone with God. Journal to Him, confessing your hidden sin, motives, agendas, and pride.

Dear God,

imagine.

As you have studied this week, how have you come to think God wants you to relate to Him? What is He chasing after in you?

Draw a picture of what you feel God is looking for in you. Use an analogy or an image that represents the concept.

deal.

Grab one or two friends who know you well and love you, and take them to dinner or coffee. (If you don't have people like this right now, start praying for God to bring them into your life.) Ask them to be "Nathans" in your life—to be truth tellers. Talk about your blind spots, sin struggles, and weaknesses. Ask them to be honest and do not defend yourself. Also talk honestly about your gifts and strengths. This will be difficult but it could also be life-changing. Afterward, journal about your experience.

People see our junk. We need to be aware of it too.

> Iron sharpens iron,
>   and one man sharpens another.

> proverbs 27:17

Conclusion

Against you, you only, have I sinned
and done what is evil in your sight.

psalm 51:4

Unless we find ourselves in the words of Psalm 51:4, we are unaware of our sin. Our limited view of sin usually involves us carrying around rulers, measuring ourselves and our sins against others. Some of us feel hopeless because our sin feels even worse than David's. But others of us believe we are okay because we just aren't that bad.

God's view of sin encompasses any unbelief, anything short of loving God with your entire mind, soul, and strength, which is the greatest commandment. Belittling Him in any way is as offensive to Him as murder or adultery, because the sin is against our holy God and Creator. As I've pointed out before, the sin is so great because we sin against Someone so great. Every single one of us does this, every single day. It's one thing to say we sin, though, and it's another thing to actually enter into the reality of that dark moment to feel the weight and sadness of what sin truly means for us.

But after the dark moments God steps in to save us despite our wreck of a life. Digging up sin is about as fun as digging up concrete, but it is necessary and worth it. To taste the forgiveness and freedom God offers is the sweetest thing this side of heaven. Grace gets real when we see our need for it.

notes

surrender :: 6

Surrender to God is not dictated by our circumstances.

Pretty Expectations

My sister Brooke had been through so much in such a short amount of time it physically hurt to think of it. Months before it all, we had walked on the beach together, analyzing how we, now in our thirties, had come so far from the entitled attitudes we carried post-college. Life was no longer made up of boxes to check on a long list of pretty expectations. We were over it. Life wasn't perfect anymore, but now more than we wanted perfection and being happy, we wanted God. But to get God we were learning to receive our lives rather than try to control them. With sand in our toes and a healthy baby girl growing in Brooke's tummy, these were the topics of our day: a God who could not be controlled, and how much we wanted more of Him. It was a beautiful day and an even more beautiful conversation.

Two months later, baby Lucy would be born to my sister and her husband in the middle of the night, already with Jesus. Nights you hold babies that don't breathe make you wonder if God is real. He seemed harder to spot in that dark hospital room than beside the waves on that bright day when my sister and I walked together. Even though we had meant every word by the ocean, we wanted to take them back that night.

God, we want to control our lives, because You don't feel safe enough.

Somewhere along the way I picked up the idea that if I loved God, He was supposed to bless me . . . in spite of every piece of evidence to the contrary. Death, sickness, divorce, infertility, and depression seem to not take into account the spiritual lives of their victims. Often it is the people I respect most who seem to be suffering the most. So it begs the question . . .

Are we willing to surrender fully to a God who may let us suffer?

And he said . . . "The LORD gave, and the LORD has taken away; blessed be the name of the LORD."

job 1:21, emphasis added

As we approach this sensitive subject, you will see God's call on David's life did not prevent him from suffering. The last seasons of David's life were filled with unfathomable hurt.

study ::

read 2 samuel 13
and
2 samuel 18:13–33

Describe the major events David saw unfold in his children's lives.

Describe what David could have been thinking and feeling.

What would you have been thinking if you had spent your life serving God and suddenly your life began to fall apart?

Jesus never promises there won't be trouble. He promises to be our peace through it.

I have told you these things, so that in me you may have peace. In this world you will have trouble. But take heart! I have overcome the world.

john 16:33 NIV

We have to lay down the false sense of entitlement we have built that God owes us a good life. Jesus was clear about what to expect here: "In this world you WILL have trouble."

Getting God

Throughout Scripture God confirms what anyone who lives on this planet should already know: that all people, even good people, suffer. The primary reason most of us live in disappointment is that we have put our hope in this life and, not surprisingly, it has failed us. Our one and only sustaining hope is that God has overcome this world and is preparing our home in the next. We certainly experience God's blessings in this life, but blessings are not promises.

Honestly, we also live in disappointment because we are not that impressed with the fact that as believers in Christ, we get God. We think He is not enough for us. We want more. Pull back from these temporary days here on earth and consider that we aren't here long. Paul says, "I consider everything [even my gains] a loss compared to the surpassing greatness of knowing Christ Jesus my Lord" (Philippians 3:8 NIV). Oh to view Christ this way, with this affection. For Paul, nothing here on earth could compare to knowing Christ.

Nothing good on this earth even compares to God's love, and no suffering compares to the suffering of being separated from God. Every human living on earth experiences common grace, the everyday participation of God in creation: the sun and the stars, and laughter and hope and babies, and coffee and gifts and fulfillment, and on and on. To truly be forsaken by God would be the definition of suffering. Those of us who have been saved by Christ will never taste this kind of suffering, because Christ faced God's wrath for us.

> He was despised and rejected by men,
> a man of sorrows, and familiar with suffering. . . .
> Surely he took up our infirmities
> and carried our sorrows,
> yet we considered Him stricken by God,
> smitten by him, and afflicted.
> But he was pierced for our transgressions,
> he was crushed for our iniquities.

isaiah 53:3, 4–5 NIV

And that is not just enough—that is more than enough. That we have God forever . . . that is more than enough.

Everyday Surrenders

Surrender does feel costly when our lives are falling apart, but surrender sometimes feels even more difficult in the mundane everyday. And God calls us to trust Him with both. Surrendering to God means we will willingly receive whatever He has for us. It could involve big things like cancer or losing our job, but usually surrender comes in the form of being content with tight budgets, or helping our roommate decide what to wear before she gets picked up for a date when we are single, or staying up with a child all night with a fever.

We mistakenly believe God is holding out on us if He doesn't give us the things on earth we most desire. But God spoke us into being, He poured out the blood of His Son, and He filled us with His Spirit. The depths of God fill the depths of us. He is withholding nothing. He gave us all of Himself. The God of universes gave every piece of Himself for us.

When we begin to see that a God like that is One we want to surrender to, when we see there is nothing more beautiful than someone whose life is God's for the taking, He takes our surrendered lives and pours them out on people who need His grace. But we must first offer Him everything and be content with however He writes our story.

Is God holding out on you?

Respond

Christ experienced the ultimate suffering of being separated from God because of our sin, so we wouldn't have to. Read as David described his own suffering and notice how it foreshadowed what Christ would suffer for us. Like David, we can be crushed, yet behind our sorrow there is always a quiet melody of hope.

Psalm 22

My God, my God, why have you forsaken me?
    Why are you so far from saving me, from the words of
    my groaning?
O my God, I cry by day, but you do not answer,
    and by night, but I find no rest.
Yet you are holy,
    enthroned on the praises of Israel.
In you our fathers trusted;
    they trusted, and you delivered them.
To you they cried and were rescued;
    in you they trusted and were not put to shame.
But I am a worm and not a man,
    scorned by mankind and despised by the people.
All who see me mock me;
    they make mouths at me; they wag their heads;
"He trusts in the LORD; let him deliver him;
    let him rescue him, for he delights in him!"
Yet you are he who took me from the womb;
    you made me trust you at my mother's breasts.

On you was I cast from my birth,
    and from my mother's womb you have been my God.
Be not far from me,
    for trouble is near,
    and there is none to help.
Many bulls encompass me;
    strong bulls of Bashan surround me;
they open wide their mouths at me,
    like a ravening and roaring lion.
I am poured out like water,
    and all my bones are out of joint;
my heart is like wax;
    it is melted within my breast;
my strength is dried up like a potsherd,
    and my tongue sticks to my jaws;
    you lay me in the dust of death.
For dogs encompass me;
    a company of evildoers encircles me;
they have pierced my hands and feet—
I can count all my bones—
they stare and gloat over me;
they divide my garments among them,
    and for my clothing they cast lots.
But you, O Lord, do not be far off!
    O you my help, come quickly to my aid!
Deliver my soul from the sword,
    my precious life from the power of the dog!
Save me from the mouth of the lion!
    You have rescued me from the horns of the wild oxen!

I will tell of your name to my brothers;
in the midst of the congregation I will praise you:
You who fear the Lord, praise him!
All you offspring of Jacob, glorify him,
and stand in awe of him, all you offspring of Israel!
For he has not despised or abhorred
the affliction of the afflicted,
and he has not hidden his face from him,
but has heard, when he cried to him.
From you comes my praise in the great congregation;
my vows I will perform before those who fear him.
The afflicted shall eat and be satisfied;
those who seek him shall praise the Lord!
May your hearts live forever!
All the ends of the earth shall remember
and turn to the Lord,
and all the families of the nations
shall worship before you.
For kingship belongs to the Lord,
and he rules over the nations.
All the prosperous of the earth eat and worship;
before him shall bow all who go down to the dust,
even the one who could not keep himself alive.
Posterity shall serve him;
it shall be told of the Lord to the coming generation;
they shall come and proclaim his righteousness to a people
yet unborn,
that he has done it.

Who are you, Lord?  What do you want for me?

In the next few projects, take time to reflect on the state of your heart and what you have learned about God in this study of David. Think about your hopes for your future as you pursue God's heart in this life and the next.

engage.

We all have expectations . . . expectations about our life, our marriage, our job, our God. And God in His mercy does let us experience joy in these things, but He gives us something so much more substantial than this short life.

Where have you unknowingly let expectations rob you of joy? Make a list below of unmet expectations in your life. Write what God says your expectations should be for this life.

	Expectations	What God Says
Relationships		
Job Opportunities		
God		
Finances		
Other		

dream.

Dream about heaven.

What will you see?

Who will be there?

What will you be doing?

Where will you live?

What do you imagine God will be like?

Then I saw a new heaven and a new earth, for the first heaven and the first earth had passed away, and the sea was no more. And I saw the holy city, new Jerusalem, coming down out of heaven from God, prepared as a bride adorned for her husband. And I heard a loud voice from the throne saying, "Behold, the dwelling place of God is with man. He will dwell with them, and they will be his people, and God himself will be with them as their God. He will wipe away every tear from their eyes, and death shall be no more, neither shall there be mourning, nor crying, nor pain anymore, for the former things have passed away."

revelation 21:1–4

act.

Did not I weep for him whose day was hard?
Was not my soul grieved for the needy?

job 30:25

Ecclesiastes 3:4 says there is a "time to weep, and a time to laugh; a time to mourn, and a time to dance." There is a time for grief and many people you know are in a season of grief. Think of a friend who is suffering.

Write your friend a letter and include passages of Psalms. Take time to hurt with this friend. Christ hurts with us and gives us space to hurt. Be the hands and feet of Christ to someone this week.

consider.

Not only that, but we rejoice in our sufferings, knowing that suffering produces endurance, and endurance produces character, and character produces hope.

romans 5:3–4

Describe a time you have suffered.

Where was God in that season?

How are you different because of that suffering?

What was your hope through that time?

Conclusion

My sister Brooke named her baby girl Lucy Hope because she knew she would see her again. And in the weeks and months that followed Lucy's death, Brooke clung to God through this verse:

> "The LORD is my portion," says my soul,
>> "therefore I will hope in him."

lamentations 3:24

The Lord is enough of a portion to fill our souls. We don't always feel full or remember He is enough. David often questioned God's presence as he suffered. But as we read how David cried out to God, we can sense his soul filling with something real and satisfying. Before long David was praising God because God was his portion. God was enough.

So my sister keeps praying to the God who let her suffer . . . she keeps handing her life over to Him and saying, "Your will be done with us." That is a beautiful thing to say to God: "You have me. Whatever you want to do with my life, I am yours."

> God is our refuge and strength,
>> a very present help in trouble.
> Therefore we will not fear though the earth gives way,
>> though the mountains be moved into the heart of the sea,
> though its waters roar and foam,
>> though the mountains tremble at its swelling.

psalm 46:1–3

notes

chased down :: 7

God chased us down through Jesus.

What do we long for more than any other thing? The holes every person tries to fill from birth till death are the needs to be known and to be loved. We chase everything trying to fill these God-given holes. He left space in us for Him. That's just plain cool. He made us incomplete without Him and yet we want everything but Him . . . so He came after us.

We had a bed that once was empty, a bottom bunk we never thought would be permanently filled. But we could not shake God's leading to fill that empty bed with a child who needed a home. After embarking on the journey toward our fourth child, one and one-half years would pass before he would fill that bottom bunk. For more than five hundred nights I would kiss my oldest son in the top bunk, look at the neatly made bottom bunk, and hurt and pray for our son who was waking up an ocean away in a little cement room with twenty-five other African toddlers.

I wanted that boy so deeply I would have swum to him.

A four-year-old with no living relatives and not one possession to his name had no idea that across the world, a mom and dad were crying and praying and spending every drop of savings to get to him. He didn't know.

God's Reach

Most of my life I've either been working hard to please God or feeling guilty for not pleasing Him. But David wasn't possessed by that struggle. Something about David's understanding of our God was different. He experienced something most of us long for more than any other thing: he experienced God's love for him. There was no measuring up, just a God who loved him and saved him.

> I waited patiently for the LORD;
>> he turned to me and heard my cry.
> He lifted me out of the slimy pit,
>> out of the mud and mire;
> he set my feet on a rock
>> and gave me a firm place to stand.
>
> psalm 40:1–2 NIV

I was in a pit, and my striving to get out only took me deeper into it. God reached in for me. God came after me. Courage and obedience and assurance and repentance come only from a God who reached into a pit to save us. They aren't things to strive after. They are the result of knowing a real God who really saved us and then moved in and settled in our souls.

David's life was remarkable only because he believed in God and the God he actually believed in was remarkable.

God

chose

adopted

filled

strengthened

enabled

convicted

restored

forgave

established

David.

God made David great. David just let Him.

And through David, God was chasing after all of us. He knit together generations to get to us. He came as an infant to get to us. He died a brutal death to get us.

study ::

read ephesians 1:3-14

What did Christ do for us?

What happened to us?

What does that mean for our lives now?

Why would God do this?

But because of his great love for us, God, who is rich in mercy, made us alive with Christ even when we were dead in transgressions—it is by grace you have been saved.

ephesians 2:4–5 NIV

Do you feel unconditionally loved by God?

Entirely New

Because of Christ, not one thing is the same. We aren't striving to be new. We are just . . . new. The old "us" died with Christ and we came back something entirely different. David lived as if it were all true. Those of us in Christ have not one bit less of God in us than David did, and God is not one bit less powerful now than He was when David was alive. We just don't live as if it were all true.

God

chose

adopted

filled

strengthened

enabled

convicted

restored

forgave

established

us.

And now we can go live out God in us, brave and obedient and repentant and humble and forgiven, because we are God's. He chased after us, not because we were worthy but because God is just that good.

Respond

God saves. David knew he was incomplete without God. David actually believed God was real and he was hopeless without God intervening.

Psalm 40

I waited patiently for the LORD;
    he inclined to me and heard my cry.
He drew me up from the pit of destruction,
    out of the miry bog,
and set my feet upon a rock,
    making my steps secure.
He put a new song in my mouth,
    a song of praise to our God.
Many will see and fear,
    and put their trust in the LORD.
Blessed is the man who makes
    the LORD his trust,
who does not turn to the proud,
    to those who go astray after a lie!
You have multiplied, O LORD my God,
    your wondrous deeds and your thoughts toward us;
    none can compare with you!
I will proclaim and tell of them,
    yet they are more than can be told.
In sacrifice and offering you have not delighted,
    but you have given me an open ear.

Burnt offering and sin offering
    you have not required.
Then I said, "Behold, I have come;
    in the scroll of the book it is written of me:
I delight to do your will, O my God;
    your law is within my heart."
I have told the glad news of deliverance
    in the great congregation;
behold, I have not restrained my lips,
    as you know, O Lord.
I have not hidden your deliverance within my heart;
    I have spoken of your faithfulness and your salvation;
I have not concealed your steadfast love and your
faithfulness
    from the great congregation.
As for you, O Lord, you will not restrain
    your mercy from me;
your steadfast love and your faithfulness will
    ever preserve me!
For evils have encompassed me
    beyond number;
my iniquities have overtaken me,
    and I cannot see;
they are more than the hairs of my head;
    my heart fails me.
Be pleased, O Lord, to deliver me!
    O Lord, make haste to help me!

Let those be put to shame and disappointed altogether
     who seek to snatch away my life;
let those be turned back and brought to dishonor
     who delight in my hurt!
Let those be appalled because of their shame
     who say to me, "Aha, Aha!"
But may all who seek you
     rejoice and be glad in you;
may those who love your salvation
     say continually, "Great is the LORD!"
As for me, I am poor and needy,
     but the Lord takes thought for me.
You are my help and my deliverer;
     do not delay, O my God!

Who are you, Lord?

What do you want for me?

reflect.

Go back to the three things you were chasing on page 22 of the Getting Started lesson.

Write them again here.

If you met God today, would you be proud these were the pursuits of your life?

May we have one pursuit. One.

Jesus.

worship.

Download a Hillsong United song, Chris Tomlin's "Amazing Grace," or U2's "40."
Listen to it in your car or while you're walking and just thank Jesus. Sing and pray and
worship a God who loves us no matter our mistakes and pursues us while we run after
everything but Him.

commit.

The consequences of God's love are great. He, in most ways, has wrecked the life I was planning to have. But He promises a better life. He promises to build stories that last forever through us and He promises to live life with us, in us and through us.

What are you
leaving behind?

What are you
moving toward?

respond.

Spend an hour with a good friend or your spouse this week and share with him or her what God is teaching you.

What has most convicted you while studying the life of David?

What did you discover you believed about God that was incorrect?

What have you learned about His character?.

How do you want to live in light of this?

Wrapping Up

That bottom bunk bed I told you about isn't empty anymore. Last night after stories and prayers and giggles, with new, broken English my African son comforted himself with this truth:

"Mom, when I was sad at the orphanage, you were working hard to get me."

I pulled him so tight and he let me. "Oh, we wanted you Cooper. So much that it hurt inside. We had to get you. While you were waiting we were chasing you down."

God has chased us down and none of our pursuits, however vain, could make Him love us less. David loved God and God loved David. Courage, obedience, belief, repentance, and surrender all flowed out of the depth of their love for each other, from the depth of their relationship. This is why we can't muster these qualities up on our own. They come from a source. The source is a relationship with God. And if we weren't so numb to those words, we would come out of our skin with excitement that this is even possible. A relationship with the God who speaks planets and souls and stars into place . . . that is unthinkable.

When I meet God, I want to face Him completely out of breath from having chased Him with these few days I have on earth. On that day, I want to have lived what I say I believe. I want to have talked to God more than I talk to anyone else. I want to have trusted God and followed Him anywhere.

May we run after God today with the same faith we will have the day our faith becomes sight. I have a feeling every other pursuit will feel futile on that day.

Let's live like God is real and heaven is coming.

For now we see in a mirror dimly, but then face to face. Now I know in part; then I shall know fully, even as I have been fully known.

1 corinthians 13:12

about the author

jennie allen

Jennie Allen's passion is to communicate a bigger God through writing and teaching. By creating raw, relational conversations about struggles and hopes, her Bible studies aim to lead women to consider truth and how it applies to their lives. She graduated from Dallas Theological Seminary with a masters in Biblical studies and is blessed to serve alongside her husband, Zac, in ministry in Austin, Texas. They have four children, including their youngest son who was recently adopted from Rwanda.

acknowledgments

I want to thank some of the people who have invested in my life and pushed me to chase God.

Fellowship Bible Church in Little Rock—thank you for raising me in my faith.

Ann Parkinson modeled passionately loved people and Jesus for me as I was growing up.

Joe White's passion for God is contagious and it lit something in me as a teenager at Kanakuk Kamps.

Michelle Bost, you showed me what discipleship looked like during my years in college through CRU. Thank you, Michelle and CRU.

Beth Moore, your passion for God showed me I wasn't crazy. And as a female teacher of God's Word, I stand on your shoulders.

Thank you for obeying God with your life and ministry.

Glenn Kreider expanded my view of God and made me fall in love with studying God in my years at Dallas Theological Seminary. Thank you Dr. K and DTS.

Karen Freisen and Gayle Clark, you keep me chasing God. You are friends and mentors at the same time.

Austin Stone Community Church—you raise the bar of what it means to follow Jesus. I run faster today because of you. Honored to be led by the most passionate and God-fearing people I know.

And of course thank you to my parents, Carolyn and Bill Stowers, and to my husband, Zac, you continue to show me God everyday! Thank you for your investment in my life.

Finally, to the many women who sat on living room floors the very first Chase and watched a mess of a girl try to figure out God, you are a part of these words. Thank you for wrestling through this with me. Thank you for chasing God alongside me.

There are too many to name. But I pray you know your faith has fallen into my life and made me see God. Thank you.

Compel [them] to come in.

luke 14:23 ESV

compelproject.com